A Shire book

Motor Car Mascots and Badges

Peter W. Card

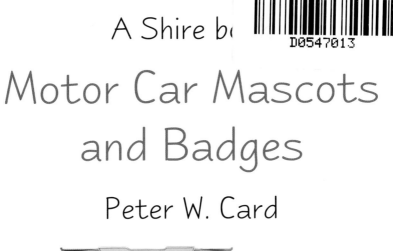

Two rare Brooklands club badges that would have been enthusiastically displayed on the cars of the members of the governing committees of both clubs. (Back) A delightfully designed first-pattern Brooklands Aero Club membership badge depicting, in enamels of five colours, a banking biplane that has just taken off from the Brooklands airstrip. Its rarity is identified by the replacement of the upper tablet, which would normally state 'Aero-Club', by a tablet announcing 'Committee', with yellow enamel lettering on a light blue background. (Front) Designed by F. Gordon Crosby in 1931, an approved-pattern Brooklands Automobile Racing Club badge. It depicts, in six coloured enamels, two cars passing beneath the Members Bridge on the Brooklands banking, but with the upper BARC tablet replaced by a 'Committee' tablet. Both badges were manufactured by Spencer & Company of London and are appropriately stamped on the rear. Given the rarity of these badges, and therefore their high value, the author fears that, unfortunately, in the future unscrupulous people will reproduce examples and pass them off as originals. Collectors are therefore warned to be on their guard.

To Pam, Julie and David.

Published in 2005 by Shire Publications Ltd,
Cromwell House, Church Street, Princes Risborough,
Buckinghamshire HP27 9AA, UK.
(Website: www.shirebooks.co.uk)

British Library Cataloguing in Publication Data:
Card, Peter W.
Motor car mascots and badges. – 2nd ed.
– (Shire album; 265)
1. Automobiles – Decoration 2. Automobiles – Trademarks
3. Automobiles – Trademarks – Collectors and collecting
4. Insignia 5. Insignia – Collectors and collecting
I. Title 629.2'62
ISBN 0 7478 0629 2

Editorial Consultant: Michael E. Ware, former Director of the
National Motor Museum, Beaulieu.

Cover: *(From left to right) A Vulcan lorry mascot with an integral radiator cap; 'Rallye Turistico Lugano 1935' – a multi-coloured enamel rally dashboard plaque; a Monte Carlo Rally Commissaire lapel badge; a figure of a little girl with a camera by C. Omerth, with an ivory face and hands on a bronze body; a Motor Corps enamelled circular badge; a British Automobile Racing Club 1912–72 Jubilee enamel dashboard plaque; a BARC multi-coloured enamel badge designed by F. Gordon Crosby; a standing Pierrot mascot by C. Omerth, with a gilt bronze finish and silver detail; a Bugatti radiator badge; a leaping tiger mascot by Brau, chromium-plated on brass; a Royal Automobile Club full member's badge dating from 1910; Mille Miglia dashboard insignia in the shape of a Mille Miglia direction indicator sign.*

ACKNOWLEDGEMENTS
The author expresses his thanks to Gordon Gardiner, John and Henrietta Boggs for
primary research material and photographs, Julie Card for access to her collection of
French mascots, and Adrian Brown for his excellent photography.

Printed in Great Britain by CIT Printing Services, Press Buildings, Merlins Bridge,
Haverfordwest, Pembrokeshire SA61 1XF.

Contents

Some motorists of the past enthusiastically decorated their cars. This Lancefield-bodied Lagonda LG45 has a Lejeune & Company 'Horse and Lucky Horseshoe' mascot fitted to the radiator cap and twenty-three car club badges fitted in front of the radiator grille. Despite the reduction in the efficiency of the radiator, various French, British, American and German badges can be seen, prominent amongst them being Der Deutscher Automobil Club and Automobil Club von Deutschland badges. One wonders if the owner was a member of every car club represented or if he simply informally collected the badges and illicitly mounted them.

Approved mascots

The human desire for individualism has been especially manifested in people's attitude towards their motor cars and their wish, from the earliest days of motoring, to embellish and personalise their vehicles. This often took the form of some kind of talisman or insignia that reflected their actual or perceived status in life. The landed gentry often emblazoned family armorial bearings on their cars, which encouraged the Inland Revenue to levy an annual two-guinea fee for the privilege; a lady driver might have a stuffed toy tied to her radiator grille; and many chauffeurs or tradesmen would encourage the saints Christopher or Bartholomew to protect their way with a brightly enamelled badge attached to the dashboard.

The first person to commission a motor car mascot was John Scott Montagu, who had a small statue of St Christopher, the patron saint of travellers, attached to the Daimler he purchased in 1899. Queen Margherita of Italy set the fashion for such mascots in the European smart set by similarly using a gilt St Christopher before she plunged into mourning after the loss of her husband in 1900.

The silver-plated standing lion mascot, as used by Queen Elizabeth the Queen Mother on her Daimler DK400 and later a DS420. Given to her chauffeur upon his retirement, the mascot has been reunited with one of Her Majesty's Daimlers, now in private hands.

A good selection of St Christopher enamelled dashboard plaques, commemoration plaques and a Vesta case with a motoring motif.

It was not until after the First World War that manufacturers realised the benefits of offering an approved mascot, either as standard equipment or as a recommended accessory. Intended to give an air of dignity and grace to the car, a mascot also made the make of the vehicle easily recognisable, and therefore helped to sell more cars.

As the motor car became more popular, less expensive to use and, in consequence, more standardised in style, so the lucky mascots, talismans and sculptures appearing on radiator caps became more outrageous and unseemly, often totally inappropriate to the vehicle they adorned. In 1910 the directors of Rolls-Royce became so alarmed at the disregard being shown for the dignity of their vehicles that they decided that a more august and exclusive mascot should be designed.

A Jules Miesse et Compagnie 'George and the Dragon' mascot, as used by the Belgian car manufacturer before the company's demise in 1926.

They commissioned the sculptor Charles Sykes to invent a suitable emblem.

Claude Johnson, the managing director of Rolls-Royce in 1910, was aware of Sykes's ability through his work for the magazine *The Car Illustrated*. When the mascot was finally announced, after several unsatisfactory designs, in March 1911, he wrote in the magazine's editorial:

> Conveying the spirit of Rolls-Royce, Mr Sykes had in mind the Spirit of Ecstasy, who selected road travel as her supreme delight and has alighted on the prow of a Rolls-Royce motor car to revel in the freshness of the air and the musical sound of her fluttering draperies.

'The Spirit of Ecstasy' set the standard in car manufacturers' approved mascots and inspired many imitations, and it continues to be the best known, remaining in constant use until the present day. Ten main variations have been manufactured since that time, and originally the *cire perdue*, or lost wax, process was used in its manufacture. It has often been claimed, quite wrongly, that early mascots were cast in solid silver. In fact, a lighter white metal was used for the early, pre-1914, mascot because the Rolls-Royce management thought the extra weight

Above: *Riley Motors believed the 'Ski Lady', announced in January 1931, epitomised 'smoothness and speed', which was 'characteristic of the art of skiing', together with the 'capacity for high speeds without effort'. Fitted to their six-cylinder models and other cars, they usually possess the registered design number on the base, RD 759377. The mascot was priced at 37s 6d and was available from Riley agents until 1937. Copies are often poorly finished, with facial definition lacking in comparison with the originals.*

'La Victoire de Samothrace' ('The Victory of Samothrace') mascot offered by Brasier Cars of France between 1920 and 1923. The inspiration for it was the discovery in the nineteenth century of a headless winged statue on the island of Samothrace in the Aegean Sea. The original statue is on show in the Louvre in Paris.

A good display of seven Rolls-Royce 'The Spirit of Ecstasy' mascots dating from the 1920s and 1930s.

of cast bronze would distort the radiator shell. After the First World War the mascots, like many others, were created from a mixture of non-ferrous metals and were usually nickel-plated to a high standard, which probably accounts for the silver epithet.

The subtle changes made to the mascot's size and shape over the years will be of interest to collectors. Because of the height of the bonnet, a lower, kneeling, female figure was registered in 1934 and introduced with the then current Phantom III, Wraiths and some 25/30 horsepower motor cars.

Collectors can also date standing examples to before or after 1928. The early models had the signature 'Charles Sykes', but post-1928 examples had just 'C. Sykes' inscribed on the base, together with 'Feb 11', which refers to the month and year of the original registration: February 1911.

Mythology

'The Spirit of Ecstasy' was not the first approved mascot, however. It is believed that the first such mascot, a figure of Vulcan, the blacksmith god, was offered in about 1903 by the Vulcan Motor Company of Southport. Various Vulcan mascot designs were created and, because the design incorporated a flat base, quite a few were also issued as 'trade gifts' and sat on the desks of Vulcan agents before the Second World War.

Other companies as well as Vulcan turned to mythology for inspiration, and also to heraldry. For instance, the Buckinghamshire company Cubitt used Cupid with his bow and quiver of arrows, and Unic used various versions of a centaur holding a bow. It was not unusual for two companies to choose the same symbol, so Gardner and Vauxhall both used the gryphon, and Guy and Pontiac both chose an Indian chief's head. This would have been confusing but for the fact that, in each case, one company was English and the other American.

In 1919 the Farman company of France began to use the Greek

Left: *This mascot was designed by P. de Soete specifically for the Belgium-manufactured Minerva Eight Cylinder motor car between 1929 and 1934. Inscribed with the designer's name, it is hollow-cast and has a very Art Deco feel.*

Right: *A 1930s 'Chef indien' ('Indian Chief') accessory mascot signed by Mady, nickel-plated on bronze, 12 cm high and mounted on a radiator cap.*

An Icarus mascot by Farman, also known as 'La Conquête de l'air'. Sculpted by Colin George, it was introduced in 1919; a larger version followed in 1921. Although manufactured in France by Contenot-Lelièvre, this example was retailed by Finnigans of London. Note the fine detail to the feathering and strength of impact. The mascot stands 16.5 cm high.

mythological figure of Icarus as a mascot in a model known as '*La Conquête de l'air*'. In its original form this was a tribute, commissioned by the French government, to the achievements of the celebrated Brazilian aviator Alberto Santos-Dumont, who, among other feats, in 1902 used a steerable airship powered by an internal combustion engine to travel from St Cloud to the Eiffel Tower and back again. The mascot was designed by Colin George (who inscribed his work 'George Colin'). Finnigans of London held the sole rights for its manufacture and retail in Great Britain and at first offered a 5 inch (127 mm) high model, but a 6^1/$_2$ inch (165 mm) version was added to the range in 1921, priced at 10 guineas.

The name Vauxhall derives from one Fulk de Breant, who, on his marriage, inherited a manor near Lambeth in London which came to be known as Fulk's Hall and which later generations corrupted to Vauxhall. His family's armorial, a gryphon (a creature half eagle, half lion), was used as an emblem by the Vauxhall Ironworks, which began car production in 1903.

A bust of Minerva, goddess of the arts and professions, was installed as a mascot by the Minerva company of Belgium. The designer, Pierre de Soete, took care to give the face of the goddess sharp, uncompromising features to allude to the solid manufacture of the car, but this resulted in a severely masculine look which left owners very confused as to the gender and status of their vehicles. Nevertheless, the original design won first prize at the *Salon de l'Automobile* held in Paris in 1921.

A Voisin Icarus mascot from the early 1920s, signed by Guiraud-Rivière, nickel-plated on brass, 12 cm high and display-mounted. Clearly a pastiche of Farman's 'La Conquête de l'Air', Colin George argued on behalf of Henry Farman that it was plagiarism; as a compromise the statue was recast as a kneeling winged man. In 1923 Gabriel Voisin's 'Icare' was superseded when he created his 'Cocotte' mascot.

The Sphinx mascot of Armstrong-Siddeley was inherited from the Siddeley Deasey company before the First World War. It is believed that the inspiration for it came from the sentinels guarding the misnamed Cleopatra's Needle, the famous obelisk on the Embankment in London, and as a result of the considerable public interest in Egyptology during the Edwardian period.

Animals

Symbols of grace, speed and elegance were eagerly sought as mascots by car manufacturers, so it is not surprising that animals often feature. Both the Ford V8 Zephyr and Lincoln motor cars used the greyhound as a mascot. One of the most attractive mascots in this category is the 'Flying Stork' of Alsace used by the Hispano-Suiza company in several interpretations. The inspiration for it was the *cigogne volante* emblem that the French flying ace Georges Guynemer's Groupe de Combat 12 used on their 200 horsepower Hispano-Suiza-engined aircraft during the First World War. The French sculptor François Victor-José Bazin was commissioned to design a mascot based on the flying stork and, until the marque's demise in 1938, it was perhaps the most magnificent of the emblems then in use. Other examples of animals were the seated hare used by Alvis on their 12/50 models; the firefly on their later Firefly model; and the eagle in flight used on their Crested Eagle of the 1930s.

A Hispano-Suiza 'Cigogne', or 'Flying Stork', mascot, c.1920, signed 'F. François Victor-José Bazin', nickel-plated on bronze, 24 cm high and mounted on a radiator cap. Reproductions are frequently found and are often so well-crafted that even some experts have difficulty in distinguishing them from originals.

The Alvis seated hare mascot. A number of versions were available from the mid 1920s to 1932. Although it is believed that Lejeune manufactured all of the mascot types, only a few seem to have been stamped 'AEL' (Augustine and Emile Lejeune). Eloise Lejeune, the daughter of Louis Lejeune, has suggested that, because the Alvis managers wished people to believe the mascots were of their own manufacture, the initials AEL were discontinued.

Below: *A symbol of love and dreams, the moon, with various cats, owls and comic characters seated on it, regularly features in accessory mascot brochures and the mail-order catalogues of such companies as Brown Brothers and the East London Rubber Company.*

Leaping cats of various types were popular, with the jaguar designed by F. Gordon Crosby in 1938 for Jaguar being the most recognisable today. It was not the first mascot for a Jaguar car, however. Before the Second World War, Jaguar marques were given the prefix SS and, in 1936, the Desmo factory of Birmingham offered an 'unofficial' leaping cat mascot for use on the SS90 and SS100 models. Another leaping cat that has generated a lot of research is the tiger used on the ill-fated MG 18/100 of 1930. Originally promoted as being a unique work, instigated by Cecil Kimber at MG for use on the planned production of twenty-five cars, investigation proves that it was in fact a Casimir Brau design and had already been listed in several French catalogues of the late 1920s as an accessory mascot, named *Panthère*.

Ford had incorporated a flying bantam

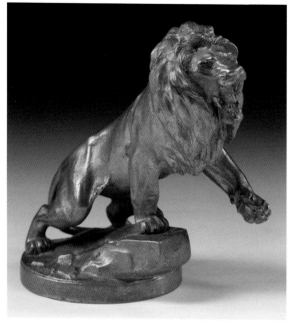

An Automobiles Peugeot lion passant mascot, a new design for the 1925 introduction of the Lion Peugeot. The sculptor was M. Marx, although the mascots are not always signed, and three sizes were available; this example has a lacquered-bronze finish and is 14 cm high.

(referred to as a quail in America) for use on their Model A car of the 1930s, and there was also a bust of Henry Ford himself available for those drivers who preferred a human icon to inspire good driving.

As motor vehicles are always spoken of as being of the female gender, so the animals incorporated as mascots are also generally assumed to be female. One major exception to this practice is the Peugeot lion. This mascot, which matured into various types, was an adaptation of the Lion of Belfort, a monument near the Peugeot factory in France. The lion had been sculpted by Auguste Bartholdi, best known as the creator of the Statue of Liberty in New York harbour. The Lion commemorates the French victory over the Prussians outside Belfort in February 1871 during the Franco-Prussian War, and it became Peugeot's emblem. Indeed, one of their earliest racing cars was called the *Lion Peugeot*. As early as 1922 the company was selling the mascot as an optional accessory. Smaller and more streamlined versions were used until 1938, when just an open-mouthed head was mounted on the 402 model, as a pale reminder of past glories. The Steyr company in Austria also used a lion emblem, as did Lion cars.

A very rare mascot in its original form was the rearing elephant that was fitted by Ettore Bugatti to his enormous Type-40 Royale model of 1927. The original and much larger bronze model was created in 1903 by Ettore's brother Rembrandt, an excellent animalier. After Rembrandt's untimely death in 1916 the elephant was kept at the car factory along with many other of its creator's works. Its adoption as a mascot certainly epitomised the Royale's qualities of strength, majesty, size and docility, but only six cars were ever produced and probably only a few dozen mascots. Consequently, the mascot has been copied and reissued several times since the Second World War and now, with the passage of time, it is difficult to distinguish between an original and a reproduction.

Initials

Some vehicle manufacturers disliked the idea of a figurative ornament fixed to their radiator caps and preferred a symbol based on the initial letter of the company. The most significant example of this is the flying B of Bentley, introduced at the London Motor Show in 1923. This took the form of an upright B with horizontal wings, incorporating fine feather detail and with a nickel-plated finish. This vintage Bentley mascot was created in two sizes and, because they are very popular with collectors today, reproductions abound. The originals can be distinguished by the B having a subtle accentuation line following the outline edge of the letter. After the takeover of Bentley by Rolls-Royce in 1931 the sales department made available, from about 1934, a

A Bugatti rearing elephant mascot.

The standing cockerel is still a very powerful emblem of French pride and no more so than when used to represent the Automobile Club de France. This example is believed to be by the artist le Courtier.

A Bentley mascot of the style dating from the 1920s. Manufactured in two sizes, original examples incorporate an accent line around the outer edge of the B motif. A large number of reproductions have been created over the years and, while they may suit some Bentley car owners prepared to risk leaving their car on the street, the dedicated collector will avoid them.

mascot comprising a forward-leaning B with a single trailing wing, for the sum of 5 guineas (£5.25). It was designed by Charles Sykes, creator of the Rolls-Royce mascot, and was eventually to develop into five variations. It appears that the company was not satisfied with the original version of the mascot and, in the February 1935 issue of *The Autocar*, they announced a competition to find a more suitable emblem, offering a prize of £50 to the winner. The design 'should not encompass birds or the female form' but what was required was 'a mascot conveying flowing lines and speed'. The competition seems not to have produced an outright winner, although two consolation prizes were awarded, and resulted in the single wing being changed to two and the base being altered. The third variation was introduced in 1939. This time the B was enlarged and sloped backwards, and the wings were extended so much that it was necessary to spin the mascot on its cap by 90 degrees to allow the engine bonnet to be opened. This mascot was allocated to the Bentley 4.25 litre overdrive model, although it often appeared on the less expensive models. The fourth type, which today is rarely found, is the Bentley Mark V mascot. This was a stylised and flowing single-wing mascot, but with an externally threaded dummy cap that screwed directly into the radiator shell. Post-war mascots were forward-leaning and reduced in size to comply with new legislation governing the size and position of projections. Other marques with an initial letter incorporated as a mascot were Austin, Daimler and Dodge Brothers.

If you have a good design, flaunt it! The Rolls-Royce mascot was such a powerful advertising symbol by the 1920s that a large showroom version of 'The Spirit of Ecstasy', as it became known, was displayed in every major Rolls-Royce showroom. Standing 36 inches (90 cm) high, original examples such as this one are rare, although copies are common.

Historical figures

Car manufacturers often named their companies, and subsequently their mascots, after historical figures such as the explorers Walter Raleigh, Hernando de Soto and Antoine de Cadillac. With its roots in the Victorian cycle industry, the Rover Company wanted an emblem that epitomised sturdiness and reliability. They chose the image of a Viking, although rather appropriately a strutting dog was briefly available in the early 1920s. The 12 horsepower model first sported a standing 'Sea Rover', as it was called, but many variations were offered by the company until 1939, when, as with so many mascots, the figure was downgraded to an enamelled shield.

From about 1928 the Trojan company used a Trojan warrior's head, intended to represent classic beauty, pluck, endurance and resolution. Today these mascots are often confused with the similar depictions used by Willeys-Knight and de Soto.

Legislation

At the end of the 1920s the government, and local councils in

A late 1920s 'Cygne sauvage' ('Wild Swan')
accessory mascot by François Victor-José Bazin
– not dangerous to the public if carefully
mounted!

particular, were alarmed at the increasing number of road fatalities, particularly those of pedestrians. As well as promoting the Highway Code in an attempt to stem the accident rate, they also wanted to legislate against mascots fitted to the front of cars, which they believed to be responsible for inflicting further injury. Various by-laws were imposed in some counties of England and Wales to restrict the use of a projection that was 'likely to strike any person in a collision'. Over subsequent years mascots were removed or refitted centrally on the bonnets (hoods) of cars but it was not until 1965 that national legislation banned them altogether from the front of vehicles registered on or after 1st February 1966. Rolls-Royce, alarmed at the prospect of not being allowed to mount their mascot as they had done for the past fifty-six years, ingeniously designed a sprung mascot that, if touched, would immediately retract into its radiator housing. Bentley, however, lost its flying B and today its mascot is an inspired flush-mounted unit, similar to that fitted to the radiators and petrol tanks of Bentleys in the 1920s.

Accessory mascots

Accessory mascots have been manufactured for almost as long as manufacturers' approved mascots, but they differ from them in two important respects: they were artistically designed to give pleasure through their ornamental effect on the vehicle and also did not represent any particular model or make of car. They have been, and continue to be, manufactured in considerable numbers in both metal and glass, and a wide variety of subject material has been used over the years to suit every pocket and taste. They can be roughly divided into four categories: sentimental, personal, humorous and bohemian.

Left: An unrecorded accessory mascot by Jean Verschneider depicting a chauffeur-boy wearing goggles and fur coat and holding a wooden pole with an American flag attached. It retains its original bronze finish, a finish that was very popular when the mascot was manufactured in c.1910.

Below: A 1920s 'Tête de cheval' ('Horse's Head') accessory mascot, signed by E. Brégeon, nickel-plated on brass, 12 cm high and display-mounted.

A 1920s 'Jeanne d'Arc au bûcher' ('Joan of Arc at the Stake') accessory mascot sculpted by Del Sarte and founded by Susse Frères of Paris, nickel-plated on brass, 18 cm high and display-mounted.

Sentimental mascots

The sentimental category includes St Christopher and St Bartholomew, the patron saints of travellers and journeymen; indeed, the early motoring pioneer John Scott Montagu, the father of Lord Montagu of Beaulieu, founder of the National Motor Museum, possessed an early depiction of St Christopher. Many rally and competitive drivers relied on the saint to secure their safety. Because so many different types have been created, a good collection of St Christopher figures, with and without the Christ-child, can make a fascinating display. Lincoln imps, horseshoes, lucky talismans and other religious figures or icons can also be included in the sentimental category.

Personal mascots

Personal mascots include animals of all descriptions, especially dogs, among which are featured bull and fox terriers, chows, Pekinese and poodles. Elephants have always been popular. They are found in an extraordinarily diverse range of poses: standing on balls, jumping out of baskets, emerging from eggs, standing on rocks, and seated. Pigs, black cats, stags and snails have also appeared in depictions which have

Above: *An accessory mascot of a racing car in the clouds. The signature of the artist, Verecke, appears on the side of the base with a deposé stamp on the opposite side. As this is an original, the front wheels spin round, whereas on reproductions they do not.*

Left: *A 1920s 'Danseur' accessory mascot sculpted by Ruffony with a foundry socle of A. N. Paris, nickel-plated on brass, 18 cm high and display-mounted as a trophy.*

A Lalique 'Tête d'aigle' ('Hawk Head') glass accessory mascot with a post-1945 intaglio signature 'Lalique France', and displayed on a mounting base.

sometimes bordered on the absurd, but all have nevertheless attracted purchasers over the years.

Humorous mascots

Some of the most charming mascots fall into the humorous category, amongst them the entertaining Robert police officer, who remains just as popular today as he was when introduced in 1914. The body and helmet were cast brass, but a dark red porcelain egg-shaped

A 1920s 'Danseuse egyptienne' ('Dancing Egyptian') accessory mascot, signed by D. Alonzo, nickel-plated on brass, 19 cm high. A smaller version was also offered.

(From left to right) A themed collection is well represented in these four different depictions of elephants: 'Tête d'éléphant' by François Bazin; 'Eléphant dressé', uninscribed; 'La Fuite de l'éléphant', by an artist signed 'RM'; 'Eléphant' by the sculptor Charles. All the mascots are similarly finished in nickel-plate and mounted on acrylic bases.

Left: 'En Quatrième Vitesse', c.1923. A dwarf riding a snail accessory mascot signed by Henri Payen, nickel-plated on brass, 8 cm high and mounted on a French radiator cap.

Below: A 1920s 'Robert the Aviator' accessory mascot signed by John Hassall, nickel-plated on brass, 12 cm high. Copies are prevalent today: original models have good detail, with the body of the aviator and aircraft having been cast separately. Although present in this example, the hand-control sticks are often missing.

head was spring-fitted, and this could be adjusted into various poses to create different facial expressions. Designed by the established illustrator John Hassall, each mascot carries his signature on the rotund waist. Three finishes were offered, nickel-plated, silver-plated and the cheaper polished brass. An aviator flying a monoplane was introduced just after the First World War and a very rare German policeman was made during the 1920s.

Old Bill is another famous mascot of this type, created by the cartoonist Captain Bruce Bairnsfather during the First World War. This jovial, moustached Tommy brought laughter to millions during the war, his antics and wry humour being depicted in the pages of illustrated pamphlets and magazines such as The Bystander's Fragments from France. After the war

A 'Robert' accessory mascot, 11 cm high, by John Hassall, who was paid a royalty for each unit sold between 1914 and the late 1920s. The helmet and body are nickel-plated brass and the head is brown porcelain with painted features.

Right: *A cold-painted bronze accessory mascot depicting Pierrot serenading the moon.*

Above left: *A cold-painted Vienna bronze owl mascot mounted on a turned silver dais and inappropriately display-mounted.*
Above right: *A 'Lièvre courant' ('Running Hare') accessory mascot, c.1925, patinated bronze, 8 cm high and display-mounted.*

homecoming servicemen attached Old Bill figures to their vehicles to remind them of one of the more cheerful products of the campaign on the Western Front. Three main types were offered: a petite example for fitting to motorcycle handlebars, a medium size for light cars and a much larger version for use on radiator caps.

Indians riding on snails and snails riding on hares exercised the imagination of a number of artists during the 1920s; indeed the French imagination for the bizarre and fanciful appears to have known no

Right: *A 1920s 'Lièvre' ('Hare') accessory mascot signed by Becquerel, nickel-plated on bronze, 18 cm high.*

Far right: *A 1930s 'Squirrel' accessory mascot sculpted by Maxime le Verrier, with a foundry socle of A. N. Paris, nickel-plated on brass.*

Below left: *A Mickey Mouse mascot, one of a number of different Mickey Mouse mascots available in the 1930s. This style has been reproduced.*
Below right: *A 1920s 'Boubou Cuisto', one of a series of four Boubou the monkey accessory mascots, signed by M. le Verrier, nickel-plated on bronze, 12 cm high and display-mounted.*

A 1920s 'Boubou à la Lanterne', Boubou the monkey holding a car headlamp, wired for electricity, signed by M. le Verrier, nickel-plated on bronze, 12 cm high and display-mounted.

bounds. In one particularly amusing series a monkey named Boubou holds a variety of everyday objects, including a lantern, soup pot, teddy bear, doll, nuts and a heavy encyclopædia. Early in the 1930s Disney characters appeared, with Donald and Pluto leading the field in collectability, and Mickey and Minnie Mouse providing a whimsical 'essential'. However, one must watch out for reproductions, particularly where the more popular characters (Mickey and Minnie Mouse, for example) are concerned.

Bohemian mascots

The bohemian category contains the most artistic designs. 'Goddess of Freedom', 'Wind Nymph', 'Nude Dancer' and 'Diving Girl' were popular with men, along with dozens of other daring and risqué poses that have been offered in the name of art. Parisian designers were very

'Eléphant à l'œuf': a mid-1920s Cardielhac mascot of an elephant emerging from an egg.

An early 1920s 'Nostradamus' accessory mascot signed by A. Loir, nickel-plated on bronze, 21 cm high.

aware that their mascot designs would be mounted on a radiator cap with its back to the driver. If the mascot included the inflaming lines of bare or scantily clad female buttocks then profitable sales, in the name of art of course, could be predicted. Lady drivers, on the other hand, being more sober in their artistic tastes, would probably have preferred the various editions of 'The Highlander', 'Marching Soldier' or 'Saluting Sailor' which were often available from jewellers and silversmiths.

Dual-purpose accessory mascots

Some accessory mascots, by accident of design, developed as dual-purpose mascots and were frequently mounted on specific models of motor car. For instance, in 1934 the Desmo company offered a leaping jaguar mascot of their own design which was somewhat flawed in that the animal had a short body, straight tail and large paws. After slow sales the company promoted it for use by the 'Owners of Jaguar Saloon Cars' after SS Cars Limited had started naming

A 1920s 'Dakotas danse' accessory mascot signed by Hentin, nickel-plated on bronze, 14 cm high and mounted on a radiator cap.

A 1925 'The Kid' accessory mascot signed by Jean Verschneider, nickel-plated on brass, 15 cm high and mounted on a radiator cap. The mascot was modelled on the Jackie Coogan character in the Charlie Chaplin motion picture 'The Kid'. Several sizes and qualities were produced.

their cars SS Jaguar from 1936. Interestingly, in modern times the mascot has wrongly been mounted on SS90 and SS100 sports cars. William Lyons, the chairman of the SS Jaguar Company, was horrified at the use of this Desmo mascot on his cars and referred to it as 'looking like a cat shot off the fence'. It was at this time that F. Gordon Crosby, the celebrated artist, was asked to design a more appropriate emblem, the design being announced in December 1938 and 'available from all dealers and agents'. The association of the letters SS with Himmler's *Schutzstaffel* in Nazi Germany became too much of an embarrassment, and the letters were removed from the company name in 1945, when the jaguar mascot became the official emblem of all Jaguar models and of the company itself. When the Auto Carrier Company (AC motor cars) brought out a car called the Greyhound in the 1930s the cars often bore a greyhound mascot. Although the Auto Carrier mascot was not officially recognised by the company itself, it was certainly given tacit approval, and a greyhound motif appeared in AC brochures of the late 1930s.

An example of the leaping cat accessory mascot so hated by William Lyons.

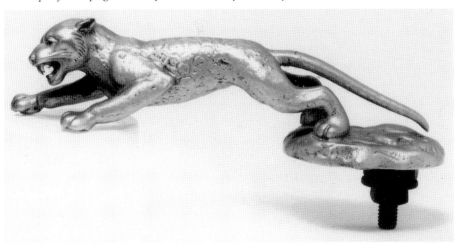

Like some manufacturers' approved mascots, some accessory mascots could be used either to decorate the car or to serve as a domestic paperweight. The Singer Motor Company's bantam mascot depicting a chicken about to take flight was also available as a desk piece, and Old Bill was often found centrally fitted to an ashtray. Vulcan standing by his anvil, in various sizes, was frequently given away as a commercial gift, and many of the biplanes and monoplanes offered as mascots were also used to embellish trophies. Guy Motors' Indian-head mascots, with their motto 'Feathers in our Cap', have been incorporated into book-ends, and the Cubist-style American Mack bulldog makes an excellent door-knocker.

Metal mascots

Most metal mascots were obtainable from a multitude of different retail outlets. Companies such as Halfords, Currys and the larger department stores always had a large and varied selection. Christmas was a busy time for mail-order firms such as Brown Brothers and Cadisch & Sons, both, like the East London Rubber Company, situated in the commercial East End of London. An inspection of the profusely illustrated catalogues of these and other companies reveals the broad range that was on offer, particularly during the 1920s and 1930s. Although some high street shops would stock a small range of the most popular models, a larger selection was available via a supplementary brochure and could be ordered direct from the manufacturer.

An early 1920s 'Singe au cerceau' ('Monkey in a Hoop') accessory mascot signed by M. Abit, polished bronze, 12 cm high and display-mounted.

Manufactured by the Jarvis Tool & Die Company, this highly detailed combination radiator cap and Willeys-Knight mascot dates from c.1928. It is finished in nickel-plating on a die-cast zinc or Mazac material. This fabric was, at the time, an excellent casting medium and was extensively used for both car mascots and toys. In later years, because of the impurities in the metal, fatigue cracks started to appear on the surface, in some cases rendering the product useless. However, the collector can eliminate further problems by keeping such mascots at a constant room temperature.

The metal used in the production of mascots varied considerably. Top quality and highly detailed mascots were created from bronze, with brass being used for the next best range. German silver, or nickel-silver, as a medium was rarely used; most manufacturers who wanted to achieve a silver finish preferred to use nickel-plate. The lead compounds, spelter and Mazac, were often utilised for the cheaper varieties. This latter compound, while perfectly acceptable at the time of purchase, possesses a soft tension that will often fatigue, particularly if stored in damp conditions. Today's collectors will recognise these mascots quite easily. They are light in weight, and the plated surface is lumpy and flaky with small cracks just visible. However, if care is exercised, good examples can be found and, working on the principle that the mascot has survived for fifty years in good fettle, with proper care it can probably be enjoyed for another fifty.

Most metal mascots could be purchased with a choice of finishes. The author's particular favourites are those nickel-plated in the old pre-1928 style, where a layer of almost pure nickel was thickly plated on to the mascot and then polished back to create a delightful straw-coloured

A Buick combination mascot and radiator cap, nickel-plated on Mazac, c.1928.

A monoplane car mascot. Created at the time of Louis Blériot's Channel crossing in a Blériot XI in 1909, this mascot has been carefully created from bronze and brass and has good detailing, including a six-cylinder rotary engine, wings, rear rudder, landing-wheels and a large propeller which spins when the car is in motion. Appealing to aviation enthusiasts, this mascot is probably one of the largest aircraft mascots ever offered.

finish. After 1928 chromium-plating was available but, while its hardness and durability were unequalled, the public preferred the restrained colour of nickel-plating to the harsh lustre of chromium. Modern nickel-plating is self-levelling and removed from the vat without the need for careful polishing. The colour is similar to chromium, which helps to identify the older mascots that have been re-plated. It can also help to establish if a mascot is a reproduction. Other finishes include oxidised, tinted, hand-painted and polished brass, the last considered inferior by the motoring public of the 1920s and 1930s.

The Lejeune family

The outstanding names amongst the numerous producers of motoring mascots are those of Emile and Augustine Lejeune, who emigrated from France in 1904. Emile was a bronze worker and artist who, with the help of Augustine, his new wife, repaired bronze ornaments and clock cases. In 1917 a sculptor friend sold them a small statuette of a naked female with arms outstretched, and Augustine, inspired by the concept, registered the design as a motor car mascot. The figurine was a success, and similar mascots of their own design followed. Their rapid success was partly due to their inspired and unique designs, with sailing boats, lighthouses, running dogs and aircraft all featuring in their output during the 1920s. They also took commissions to produce mascots for Brown Brothers, Finnigans and Desmo, and their enthusiasm for the business was unbounded. Distribution then, as today, was an important factor in the growing commercial success of a small company. It made good business sense to engage retailing companies like Halfords, Shaw &

Designed by Charles Paillet and manufactured by Augustine and Emile Lejeune in London, the 'Indien à l'escargot' ('Indian on a snail') dates from the early 1920s.

A 1930s 'Marabout' ('Stork') accessory mascot signed by Artus, nickel-plated on bronze, 15 cm high and mounted on a radiator cap.

Kilburn, Alfred Dunhill and Harrods. Later, provincial department stores, such as Beales of Cheltenham and Heelas of Reading, sold Lejeune manufactured goods under their own name. The quality of the sculpting was such that the silver retailers Aspreys of London's Bond Street and Mappin & Webb often sold the same figurines as ornaments and desk pieces. Emile also engaged the services of some of his French compatriots, including the artist François Bazin, who had designed the Hispano-Suiza 'Flying Stork' mascot, and Charles Paillet, whose award-winning designs for animals were unparalleled.

Throughout the 1920s about a hundred and thirty designs appeared. The letters AEL, an abbreviation for Augustine and Emile Lejeune, appear on many of their creations, although by no means all of them. For example, when Alvis commissioned designs for their famous hare and, later, the various designs of their eagle mascot, no recognition of the source of manufacture was allowed, possibly because, like Rolls-Royce, the company wanted the public to believe that they alone were worthy of creating the precious company mascot. Interestingly, while Rolls-Royce prided themselves on

Two male golfer mascots offered by Desmo of Birmingham (later of Brierley Hill in Staffordshire). The chromium-plated example on the left dates from the late 1930s and the example on the right depicts a golfer in plus-fours, crafted in the style of a famous early 1930s photograph of Edward, Prince of Wales. Both mascots are stamped 'Desmo' and were manufactured by Lejeune for Desmo to retail.

making their own mascots, in the 1950s they also asked the Lejeune company to make up a few Rolls-Royce 20 horsepower mascots in order that they could satisfy requests from 'our respected older customers'.

At the end of the 1920s thirty men and boys were employed at Lejeune's modern foundry at Kensal Rise in London, and another twenty staff at the salerooms and offices at London's Great Portland Street. By 1929 the company was being described as 'the world's largest motor car mascot manufacturer' and, while they were not the only company in this trade in England, the number of registered designs they lodged with the Patents Office bears testament to their industry.

When the Lejeunes separated in 1929 and Emile returned to his native France, Augustine carried on the business with verve. The chromium rage of the 1930s inspired her and the staff to new heights of flamboyance. The company exhibited at many of the European motor shows and salons and, amongst other awards, won a prize in Paris for a French bulldog. However, plagiarism was a hazard, and all of their more popular designs were imitated from time to time. As quality of manufacture often gave way to profit, identification of these rogue mascots is easy. Modern dealers are more than aware of how important

Louis Lejeune (1908–69), the son of Augustine and Emile Lejeune.

fine detail and quality of manufacture are to the collector, so original but sub-standard mascots can be quite inexpensive when offered. Lejeune also created presentation plaques and models of aircraft, boats and sports-related motifs of every kind. Often wrongly described as mascots today, they were never intended to be used as such.

The Lejeunes had a son, Louis, born in 1908. He worked alongside his mother during the 1930s, taking administrative control from 1933. After the Second World War there were few orders and the company fell into debt. In the post-war age of austerity, and with changing radiator styles, the demand for mascots almost disappeared. The boating and polo set gave some respite, and the odd order from Rolls-Royce to supply 'The Spirit of Ecstasy' mascot helped to keep trade alive. Distributors such as Harrods and shops in London's Burlington Arcade demonstrated that emblems were still in demand by the wealthy, particularly when the quality of the product was beyond doubt. The company traded as Louis Lejeune after the war but, when Louis died in 1969, his elderly mother once again took charge, along with Eloise, Louis's widow. The now much smaller company continued under their joint leadership until Augustine's death in 1977.

As an aid to identification, collectors should be aware that mascots manufactured before 1940 often bore the letters AEL stamped into the base. On mascots manufactured after 1933 LL is sometimes stamped but after 1945 the inscription 'LL Mascots, England' appears. From 1978, when David Hughes purchased the company, mascots were issued bearing the words 'LL Ltd. Made in England', so that purchasers would be in no doubt that, although made from the original company moulds, they were modern.

The name of Desmo regularly appears on motoring accessories, including lamps, motor clothing and mascots. Originally called Clayrite Limited, the company was named after its founder, Howard Clayton-Wright. It changed briefly to Dekla in 1922 and, after financial difficulties, accepted an injection of cash from Harris & Sheldon of Stafford Street, Birmingham, to form a new company. Their objective was 'solely to trade in the accessory market selling high quality British manufactured goods'. Under the trade name Desmo, derived from the names of Clayton-Wright's children, and with their financial backing, the company's buying power was such that it was able to commission mascots for selling under its own brand name. Desmo continued to offer Lejeune-manufactured mascots into the mid 1960s.

Motor meters

An interesting variation on the accessory mascot was a decorative engine temperature gauge fitted on the radiator cap. Appearing just before the First World War, this dual-purpose device bridged the gap between a simple radiator cap and the radiator-cap-mounted mascot. In the first decades of the twentieth century it was necessary to know the temperature of engine cooling systems as they were crude by today's standards and susceptible to overheating. A number of different devices were invented to monitor the temperature of the engine and display it to the driver. All comprised a probe immersed into the radiator, a threaded cap and a measuring gauge above, and all were generically known as 'motor meters'.

The best-known manufacturer of temperature gauges in the United States was Boyce, who had a factory in New York and whose gauges were also manufactured under licence in Britain by Benjamin Electric Limited of Tottenham, London. Their device was known as the Boyce Moto Meter, although it is usually inscribed 'Motometer'. It consisted of a simple thermometer with coloured alcohol in a glass tube which, against 'cool' to 'boiling' inscriptions, told the driver at a glance the temperature of his water. The Moto Meter was so successful that some companies copied the device and patent infringement battles were fought over its manufacture. The problem was caused by the fact that the Moto Meter patent related to the measurement of water vapour in the header tank

A combination winged cap and Boyce Moto Meter finished in nickel plating, c.1927. Inscribed 'Design Pat. Chrysler 6-3-24', it was designed by Oliver H. Clark. Manufactured in zinc alloy and brass, it was available in different sizes for different model cars. This example has a Chrysler disc insert.

A combination nickel-plated 'Capitol Cap', with a White House motif design as its radiator cap catch, a Boyce 'Junior' Moto Meter with an Oldsmobile disc insert fitted, together with a topper designed by L. V. Aronson. This example, representing the Elks Fraternal Organization, is dated 1923.

and not, as other patents suggest, in the water itself.

In Britain one of the most popular temperature-indicating devices was manufactured by Wilmot or, after 1928, by Wilmot-Breeden. Originally named the 'Wilmot all-British Calometer', after 1926 it was renamed the 'Calormeter'. This small change in name was made at the request of Autovac, who feared possible confusion with their 'Galometer', an instrument they manufactured for measuring petrol consumption. The design was based on the bimetallic principle, where two pieces of metal with different heat conductivity moved a ratchet device to activate a pointer, which indicated the temperature changes.

A mascot featuring the Automobile Club of North France; a two-dimensional depiction of the French cockerel fixed to the front of a Boyce Moto Meter. The rear view shows what the driver would have seen from his seat; the alcohol-filled thermometer and printed datum lines give a guide to the working temperature of the engine.

Left: *A combination Chevrolet radiator cap, Moto Meter and topper, c.1926. The cap possesses a stylised eagle head, which releases the cap so that the radiator can be filled. The Boyce Moto Meter has a Chevrolet disc insert and mounted on top of the Moto Meter is a topper attachment depicting a swimmer. The topper is marked 'Jantzen Knitting Mills Portland Ore.', and was an advertisement or possibly a trade gift for this famous swimwear manufacturer.*

A Boyce Moto Meter with a Cadillac heraldic motif on the black datum plate.

The success of these 'motor meters' was such that motor-car companies such as Ford, Nash and MG offered their own 'motor meters' with the company logo engraved either in the shielding glass or on the datum gauge.

The Moore Motor Semaphore temperature meter used a green and red disc to indicate motor temperature. There was a hole on each side of the meter that would show a green disc if the motor was cool. The device would rotate as the engine temperature increased, causing the red disc to move into the other hole, showing half green on one side and half red on the other. All red on one side indicated an overheated engine.

As the use of motor meters grew, small decorative sculptures, or motor meter 'toppers', started appearing. A mainly American phenomenon, these were well-crafted miniature mascots that could be attached to the meter to make the device more attractive and distinctive. The small holding screws of the motor meter were simply unscrewed and the mascot bracket fitted. The mascots ranged from birds, animals and female figures to the insignia of fraternal organisations and professional bodies. Many were manufactured by The Art Metal Works, run by L. V. Aronson in Newark, New Jersey, and they are often dated.

In addition to the toppers there were many other after-sale accessory mascot attachments that could be mounted on the radiator cap below the meter. These were manufactured by companies such as the Faith Manufacturing Company of Chicago, the Irving Florman Company of

An accessory mascot by L. V. Aronson finished in nickel-plating on pewter, and dated 1922. L. V. Aronson traded as The Art Metal Works in Newark, New Jersey, and manufactured novelty items, mascots, radiator attachments and cigarette lighters (this sideline later becoming the Ronson Corporation).

Below: *'Felix the Cat' was created in 1919 by Pat Sullivan as an animated cartoon to 'soften' the harsh reality of the Paramount Studios cinema newsreels. Pre-dating the popularity of Mickey Mouse by almost ten years, the character achieved worldwide recognition throughout the 1920s and 1930s and several motor car mascots were produced in his image. This example is less spherical than the original concept and therefore probably dates from the mid 1930s. Finished in cold-painted enamels on bronze, it is a typical example of an attractive mascot for the collector – ancillary history, good original condition and pleasing to the eye.*

New York, and Neal Tanquary of Los Angeles, California, and ranged from car nameplates of the different vehicle manufacturers to club insignia, Masonic emblems, doctors' badges and engraved initials dials. There were also special discs bearing the car dealer's name and address.

Although popular during the 1920s and 1930s, when an internal water temperature gauge was not fitted as standard equipment, external thermometers were phased out as cars became more sophisticated, and by 1939 almost all cars were fitted with a dial mounted on the dashboard.

Glass mascots

Mascots made of glass were among the most spectacular produced, and the most innovative designs were those created by the Lalique factory in France. Born in 1860, René Jules Lalique was a trained jeweller who discovered the artistic merits of moulded glass in about 1890. Initially he produced fanciful household goods, small decorative devices and dressing table accoutrements in the Art Nouveau style that found much favour during the last decade of the nineteenth century. It was not until 1925 that Lalique turned his attention to *bouchons de radiateur*, or radiator stoppers, when he was commissioned to design a glass mascot for the Citroën company's Cinq Chevaux-Vapeur model. The pleasing result was a daring display of ingenuity, depicting five horses in bas-relief, and it was so uniformly popular that elegant French society used this device on country and town cars of every size and distinction. Over thirty further designs in the then highly fashionable Art Deco style were developed during the next six years. These ranged in appearance from a prancing fox to the erotic 'Chrysis' and '*Vitesse*' female nudes. Some of these mascots were offered in coloured glass rather than clear, Lalique's catalogue listing a choice of green, electric blue, mauve and grey.

Glass mascots were criticised by purists who disliked their overt

Left: A Lalique 'Saint-Christophe' ('St Christopher') glass accessory mascot c.1930, with the intaglio signature 'R Lalique France', mounted on an illumination base, 15 cm high.

Below: A 'Sanglier' ('Wild Boar') charcoal-coloured glass mascot, c.1929, with an intaglio signature 'R. Lalique', 10 cm high. A good example of a mascot that doubled as a décor item.

A 'Coq nain' glass mascot with an intaglio signature 'R. Lalique France', c.1928, 20 cm high. These mascots are usually offered in clear glass, but coloured glass mascots are eagerly collected and command high prices. Unscrupulous dealers have been caught microwaving clear glass examples to achieve a colour tint before selling them to the unsuspecting public.

opulence, particularly when illuminated from below. Breves Galleries in London were highly successful in marketing the mascots during the 1930s, providing fantastic displays at art fairs, in hotel lobbies and at major social events. The most common method of mounting the mascot was to attach it to a radiator cap, but another method was to set the ornament further back on the bonnet, or sometimes on the scuttle, just in front of the windscreen. Breves Galleries created a special mount for illuminating the mascot. This took the form of a nickel-plated base incorporating a bulb and coloured filters in red, green, amber and so on. When switched on through the dynamo system, a warm glow of light would illuminate the glass and the light would become more intense as the speed of the vehicle increased.

Other companies also manufactured glass mascots. H. G. Ascher Limited of Manchester, trading as Red Ashay, imported a series of clear and frosted glass mascots from Czechoslovakia. A large number of different designs were offered. Some historians delight in comparing these mascots with those of Lalique and, to be fair, several did share the same design principle. On the other hand, many of the designs were brilliantly inspired and unique to the company. About twenty-five models were available throughout the 1930s, ranging in price from 42 to 136 shillings each.

A Red Ashay 'Racing Driver' glass accessory mascot, mounted in an illumination base with a colour filter activated by the four-bladed propeller at the front.

A Red Ashay horse's head glass mascot mounted on an illumination base. The electrical bayonet clip plug can be seen fitted at the rear.

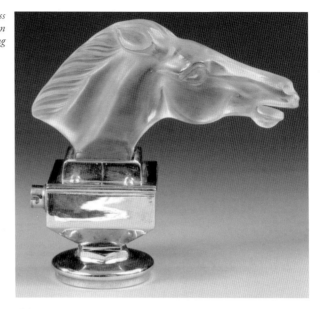

A female head with flowing hair makes an interesting comparison with Lalique's famous '*Victoire*', and a kneeling nude bears a striking resemblance to another Lalique figure, '*Vitesse*'. The Red Ashay 'Butterfly Girl', a standing woman with full-length flowing wings, was an inspired design, and the entwined 'Lovers' is as popular today as in the 1930s. Red Ashay mascots could also be supplied with illumination bases, usually of square form with catchment shoulders held down by countersunk screws. The collector should beware of reproductions. When visiting Prague, the writer came across a number of art shops selling the more common models very cheaply, these possibly having been created from the original moulds, which probably accounted for their lack of detail and inferior general finish. Unfortunately, they have been passed off as originals, even by multi-national auction houses.

The Lalique company has re-issued some of the original mascot designs. Those to look out for are the perch, the large cockerel, the hawk's head, Saint Christopher and the leaning-back nude, 'Chrysis'.

A Red Ashay 'Lovers' glass accessory mascot, mounted on a display base and attached to a radiator cap.

A 'Victoire' satin and frosted glass mascot by René Lalique. Registered as a design in April 1928, it possesses the correct intaglio 'R. Lalique France' signature. Because of chipping to the hair, many of these mascots have been ground to disguise the damage. An easy way to tell if the mascot has been shortened is to measure the distance from the nose to the tip of the hair; it should be 25.6 cm.

Always double-check originality before you purchase, as an honest dealer who values his reputation will not mind if you obtain independent advice before you part with your money.

Two Frenchmen, Maurice-Ernest Sabino and André Hunebelle, both manufactured high-quality opalescent glass figures which doubled as mascots and these, in the light of the high prices obtained for Lalique, are becoming very collectable.

A 'Comète' ('Comet') clear glass mascot by René Lalique, clearly displaying the correct signature.

Badges

Club membership, if only to prove an alliance with a special-interest group or society, is no better represented than in the proud display of the club badge upon a vehicle. Car badges fall into two main categories: badges supplied by motor car clubs to their members for attaching to their vehicles, and corporate badges, representing a trade, interest group or organisation.

Club badges

In the very early days of motoring most car owners devoted their energies to keeping their vehicles running and had little time to consider the benefits of club membership. The first British attempts at forming a club were the Self-Propelled Traffic Association in 1895 and The Motor Club a year later, both clubs being short-lived. As vehicles became more reliable, and longer and longer journeys were undertaken, so the need for a supporting body to look after the interests of motorists became indisputable. The inventor and motoring experimentalist Frederick Simms founded the Automobile Club of Great Britain in 1897 and incorporated Ireland in 1898 (ACGBI). He also founded the Society of Motor Manufacturers and Traders. Indeed, it was often said that he founded the British motor industry itself. The ACGBI expanded quickly and in 1907 received royal recognition when King Edward VII, the 'Motoring Monarch', agreed to become its first patron. It was thereafter called the Royal Automobile Club.

The new full member's badge was a spectacular design consisting of a spoked motor wheel with the King's crown

An Automobile Club de France full member's badge, c.1910, nickel-plated, with the French flag and the colours of the ACF crossed.

(From left to right) A Brooklands Automobile Racing Club badge suitable for grille mounting; an Austin Healey Club badge depicting a profile of Warwick Castle and Union Flag below; a '75 Years of Morgan (1909–1984)' celebration badge; a Jaguar Drivers' Club Millennium Celebration badge, one of a limited edition of a thousand.

(From left to right and top to bottom) A Royal Automobile Club Associate's badge for Scotland; a pre-1952 full member's badge; a Professional Golfers Association badge; an early polished brass AA badge, numbered 6144; a Rolls-Royce chauffeur's lapel badge in its box; a rare nickel-plated AA badge, numbered 2447; a Rolls-Royce Enthusiasts Club badge; a Rolls-Royce Owners Club badge; a pre-1910 AA committee member's badge; a Silverstone Club badge.

Two examples of the large Royal Automobile Club full member's badge. Numbered A610, the right-hand example possesses a hollow wheel and split wings at the base and was manufactured by Elkingtons of Birmingham c.1907. The left-hand example is similar but less detailed. The wheel is cast from the solid and Mercury's wings are not split. This badge dates from a period of re-issue in the 1920s.

above and a raised profile of the King at the centre, the whole unit supported by a winged torso of the god Mercury, messenger of the gods. The reverse, however, bore a peculiar device which is supposed to represent the centre portion of the Union Flag. This method of displaying the British national flag has no authority whatsoever, and it is just as well that, when the badge is fitted to a vehicle, courtesy requires that the King's head should face forward. This early full member's badge stands nearly 8 inches (20 cm) high and continued to be offered, albeit with several changes, until the mid 1920s. Such is the success of the design that a similar but smaller full member's badge can still be purchased from the RAC today. The full member's badge of the RAC takes precedence over all other clubs and, when fitted to a vehicle in use on British roads, it is always placed on the off-side of the car with the King's head to the front. Etiquette demanded that while motoring abroad an owner should reverse the badge to show the Union Flag.

The other major British motoring club is the Automobile Association. The AA was founded in June 1905 and, from March 1906, it produced the first official badge to be displayed on cars. The first version of the badge was a plain circle with two entwined As in the centre. Early examples bear the impressed signature of the club's first secretary, Stenson Cooke, and today these badges are known colloquially as 'Stenson Cookes'. A little later, towards the end of 1906 and after the first thousand or so had been manufactured, the word 'Secretary' was added.

The Motor Union was formed in 1902 to lobby for road improvement and supporting regulations. The MU introduced a badge in 1907

A rare copy of a Driver's Certificate of Competence, as issued by the Automobile Association & Motor Union in 1920, certifying the driver as 'having been examined and found to be competent to drive a motorcar', albeit driving tests were not statutory until 1934.

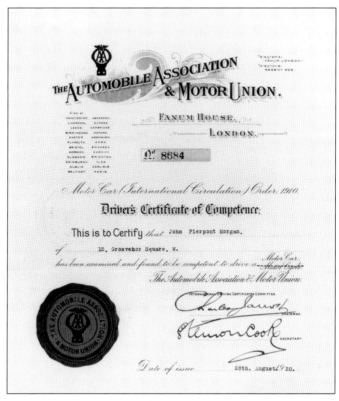

comprising an elaborate M above a small spoked wheel with a stretched letter U in its centre. A pair of wings was added as a decoration in late 1907 and, after the club amalgamated with the AA in 1910, this feature, together with the elongated style, was incorporated into a new AA badge from 1911. Being of an elegant but simple design and manufactured from sheet brass, these badges are easy to reproduce, so collectors should beware of modern copies.

From its formation the AA also catered for motorcycle riders, for whom it produced smaller versions of the car badge. In May 1914 a novel idea for use on the motorcycle badge was borrowed from the Cyclists' Touring Club. A heart-shaped attachment was designed to fit between the two entwined As; on this was inscribed in small letters the date of membership, and thus it revealed at a glance whether one was a fully paid-up

Although the Motor Union badge was introduced in 1907, the AA complained about infringement of copyright. The MU modified its badge later that year by adding separately fitted wings.

member or not. Only two hearts were produced, blue for 1915 and red for 1916.

Of the general club badges quite a number are shield-shaped, chosen perhaps because of an imagined kindred spirit between early motoring competitors and the knights of old. The Brooklands Automobile Racing Club (BARC) badge is of this shape. The club was incorporated in 1912, five years after the Brooklands racing track was opened near Weybridge, Surrey. In 1931 F. Gordon Crosby designed the popular badge now associated with the club. The design is of two racing cars speeding beneath the Members' Bridge at the Brooklands track. Using only five coloured enamels, these badges are regarded as among the most attractive ever produced. The standard full member's badge had the letters BARC emblazoned at the top, but the most sought-after are those awarded to individuals who achieved speeds of 120 mph or 130 mph on the Brooklands outer circuit. Only eighty-four of the 120 mph and seventeen of the 130mph badges were awarded and each had the appropriate tablet on the top of the standard badge in place of BARC. The driver's name and, usually, the recorded speed were engraved on the rear and badges were also awarded retrospectively for speeds achieved before 1931. The BARC closed in 1962 and collectors are warned that reproductions are currently being manufactured.

The Junior Car Club (JCC) served the racing interests of cycle and light car owners from 1919 until after the Second World War, when it

A complete collection of Brooklands Automobile Racing Club members' and guest badges dating from 1907 to 1941 makes a colourful display, however arranged.

A well-detailed, silver-gilt finished British Racing Drivers Club presentation entrance plaque for the 1936 Brooklands 500 Miles Race. Superbly crafted by George Collins of London, it is inscribed 'A. Von Der Becke'. A rewarding part of collecting such badges is that background research into the race, racetrack and entrants can give an extra dimension to the artefact; as it turns out, only seventeen cars were entered in the event, and it is likely that only seventeen plaques were awarded.

Right: A Brooklands Automobile Racing Club 120 mph badge, as awarded to Norman Black for travelling the Brooklands racetrack at over 120 mph in a 2.3 litre Alfa Romeo on 22nd September 1934. Although the badge was re-enamelled in 1990, a documented record of its history, which will help demonstrate its integrity if it is ever sold, has been retained by the owner.

Below: (From left to right) The Brooklands Aero Club badge was offered through the 1932 year book at a cost of a £1 'loan charge', the club having been revived in 1930; the SS Car Club, a rare badge inscribed 'Founder'; a badge for the Junior Racing Drivers Club, formed to encourage amateurs who did not own a racing car to 'experience high speed motoring' at the Brooklands racetrack (three categories of membership were offered, Racing, Country and Associate).

Brooklands Automobile Racing Club membership badges for 1910, 1911, 1912 and 1914 in their original delivery boxes. The boxed set comprises a circular member's badge with an attached cord for feeding through a buttonhole, together with two guest brooches. The issue number appears both on the lid of the box and stamped on the rear of each badge.

joined forces with the BARC. It had a rectangular badge bearing a diamond, with the words 'Junior Car Club', and a pair of ornamental wings to each side.

Clubs that are linked with counties or cities usually incorporate the coat of arms of the area, or some heraldic emblem borrowed from it, in the design. The best-known badges in this category are the RAC association badges that were introduced in 1908. Many regional car clubs were allowed to affiliate to the RAC and thereby provide their members with the benefits of belonging to a local car club, so enjoying the camaraderie of local membership together with the advantages of

(From left to right) A rare grille-mounting Royal Air Forces Association enamelled badge, a pre-1953 Civil Service Motoring Association car badge, and a real Automovil Club de Espana (Royal Automobile Club of Spain) grille-mounted car badge.

membership of a national club with nationwide facilities. In its original form the association badge was circular, with the words *Royal Automobile Club Associate* around the circumference. The Union Flag was placed at the centre instead of the King's head, it having been understood that the use of the royal profile was intended as a single favour conferred exclusively upon the original RAC. To replace the Union Flag, a colourful, sometimes artistic, medallion with motifs appropriate to the club's locality could also be used. The Crystal Palace Automobile Club's medallion incorporated a representation of the glass palace; the South Wales and Monmouth Club displayed the red Welsh dragon, and the Coventry and Warwickshire Motor Club exhibited the 'three tall spires' to which Tennyson referred in his poem about Lady Godiva. The eighty or so different varieties are very popular with collectors and make a wonderfully colourful display.

The Order of the Road Club was incorporated in 1928 by the then secretary of the BARC, the forward-thinking John Morgan. He also designed the splendid club badge, a depiction of the English rose with red polychrome enamel petals and a central entwined 'OR' in blue enamel against a white background. It was manufactured by Spencer's of Birmingham, perhaps the best exponents of the art. The maxim of the club was 'Road Safety and Courteous Driving'. To promote longevity of membership, members could claim a year plate quoting the number of years as a driver and, later, a rank plate was offered, with four levels of membership – Member, Commander, Knight Commander or Knight Grand Cross – depending on the number of good driving years to one's credit. The club merged with the Guild of Experienced Motorists in 1994 and, with a current membership of sixty thousand, remains a force for good on the road.

The Silverstone Club, inspired by John Taylor and incorporated in 1965, was a club for enthusiasts of motor competition at the Silverstone racing circuit. The club badge was manufactured by Marples & Beasley. It is a clever design that includes, in white enamel, the old outer racing circuit, a polychrome green centre representing the fields of

(From left to right) A Silverstone Club badge offered by the supporters' club, which started in 1965; a 1956 Rally des Alpes car badge; a Royal Automobile Club Queen Elizabeth II Silver Jubilee celebration badge from 1977; a Brooklands Aero Club badge; and a National Motorists Association badge manufactured by Collins of London (membership benefits included free emergency servicing, legal representation and discounted Lloyds of London vehicle insurance).

(From left to right) A 1981 Monte Carlo Rally entrant's badge; a Brooklands Automobile Racing Club badge, dating post-1946 (the original club was incorporated in 1912 and, after the demise of the Brooklands track, changed its name to the British Automobile Racing Club); a Sports Car Club of South Africa badge, clearly showing a polychrome gold background; a Rolls-Royce Owners Club of Australia badge from the 1960s, manufactured by K. C. Luke of Melbourne; a rare Rolls-Royce and Bentley Owner Driver Club car badge, with deep red polychrome enamelling and well-crafted wording and motifs.

Northamptonshire, and the British Racing Drivers Club shield above the name. Because of the continuing popularity of Silverstone, good examples command three-figure sums today.

Corporate badges

For almost the whole of the twentieth century and into the twenty-first a large range of club badges has been distributed. Indeed, it is quite probable that over three thousand British clubs have issued a badge of one type or another, so that today there is a plentiful supply of often obscure, sometimes colourful and usually well-manufactured badges for the enthusiastic collector. The halcyon days of motoring were the 1930s and it has been estimated that during this period more than fifteen hundred clubs were in existence, each having one or more styles of club badge. All were passionately displayed, rather too keenly in some cases, as some owners would often mount badges on the rear of the vehicle as well as the front. Corporate clubs include such august bodies as the National Guild of Telephonists, the Canine Defence League and the Royal School of Church Music. The Women's Motor Racing Associates Club, colloquially named the Doghouse Club, was co-founded in 1962 by Bette Hill, the wife of Graham Hill, the racing driver. The club's charity fund-raising was legendary during the 1960s and 1970s. Collecting badges in this category can lead to some enjoyable research. As an example, the writer found a badge with the applied scripted letters 'RCS' against a crimson background. After research into several imaginative suggestions and blind alleys, it was discovered to be the badge of the Retired Clergy Society.

Manufacturing companies, in the interests of staff harmony, often sponsored their own motoring clubs. Companies such as Rotax Accessories, British Aerospace and Brighton Beach Attendants each instigated their own club badge. Badges incorporating a national flag are usually very colourful, and that of the British Monte Carlo Competitors

Club is an example, being a shield divided into quarters and incorporating the Union Flag and the shield of Monaco. The New Zealand Motor Racing Drivers Association had a small image of New Zealand and the letters NZMRDA on the outer edge. The Midland Car Club's badge shows a rising sun, celebrating Sunrising Hill, the hill-climbing venue in Warwickshire.

There are also one-make clubs. Some were sponsored by the manufacturer (as with Standard, MG, Morris and Ford). Others are long-established owners' clubs, which serve the particular social and spares needs of their membership (as with marques such as Alvis, Bentley, Bugatti and Jaguar).

Although car badges were once a familiar feature of motoring, today they are seldom seen and those that are are usually fitted to working commercial vehicles like motorised horse boxes and four-by-fours. The decline of the popularity of the badge has much to do with the aerodynamic nose arrangements of the modern car, the increasing likelihood of car park theft and the arrival of the plastic windscreen sticker.

Above: *(From top to bottom) An Allard Owners Club badge; a Bugatti Owners Club badge; a Nurburgring car badge celebrating the silver jubilee of the racetrack in 1952; a Jersey Motor Car and Light Car Club badge.*

A '20hp Ghost' badge, the design imitating the Rolls-Royce radiator badge, with pre-1933-style red enamels. Contrary to popular belief, the alteration of the Rolls-Royce badge colour from red to black was not in deference to the death of Henry Royce in 1933 but simply reflected the changing fashion for more sedate, black cars and the mood of the era.

While the author's penchant is for themed collecting, with a little imagination it is always possible to assemble an equally interesting collection of varied, good-quality mascots.

Notes for the collector

Any collection, large or small, that has been assembled with enthusiasm and understanding will always please. Quality, not quantity, should be your maxim, and primary research your aim. The writer has enjoyed many worthwhile collections laid out carefully in the top drawer of a wooden chest, each badge neatly labelled and dated, with notes describing where the badge was acquired and detailing its history. On the other hand, rows and rows of glass cabinets full of very rare and expensive badges and mascots can be wearisome, especially when the only desire of the owner appears to have been to accentuate his wealth. Collectors are recommended to concentrate their collection around a single theme, period or type. Specific badge and mascot manufacturers make an interesting theme and a collection based on an esoteric subject like Pierrot and Pierrette have proved to be effective. Bear in mind, however, that a collection of René Lalique glass mascots in a skilfully illuminated showcase may look stunning, but its magnificence will be matched by the high cost of purchase.

Reproductions and forgeries

Because the values of some of the rarer mascots and badges have risen sharply, modern reproductions are being manufactured and in some cases deliberately passed off as originals. To avoid being cheated, collectors should follow two golden rules when considering the purchase of an item.

First, from whom are you buying? Auction houses often conduct sales of automobilia where badges and mascots are offered. However, just because the auction house has an international reputation, it does not mean that the products they offer are always correctly catalogued, or that the item is as honest as the sometimes arrogant staff 'experts' report it to be. It is far better to purchase from a dealer with a long-standing reputation to uphold, who will stand by his hard-earned expertise, authenticate the item's approximate age and provenance and give you a receipt highlighting those fundamental issues. If in any doubt, it is advisable to find an alternative supplier.

Second, what is the finish? As most metal mascots could be purchased with a choice of plated finishes, these features should be carefully considered. Before 1928 the only standard finishes available were straw-coloured nickel-plate and what was sometimes described as 'oxidised', this being a finish created by immersing very hot bronze into a vat of linseed oil. Chromium-plating, with its hardness and durability, was universal throughout the 1930s, although it was not in common

Various high-quality dashboard-mounted enamel competition and club badges.

In today's frenetic world, it is difficult to understand the slower and more dignified pace of the 1920s and 1930s when the protocol of motoring demanded that when a 'motor vehicle was active in an area of commerce', the vehicle's mascot was not displayed 'lest it would cause anxiety amongst the populace'. Instead, a 'Town Cap should be employed as a replacement to the mascot', as featured on this Penman-bodied Rolls-Royce 20 horsepower of 1926, and, once the vehicle had left the suburbs, the mascot was remounted for the onward journey.

commercial use until 1928. This, like all finishes, will deteriorate with time and will begin to show its age after a few years even if it has never been mounted on a vehicle. This wear is a positive attribute, and it is better to purchase a mascot showing the wear that only time can inflict rather than an old mascot that has been newly plated, where it is likely that some details will have been lost on the polishing mop before plating. If a dealer suggests that the reason for a mascot's superb condition is the result of careful storage, regard all his statements with suspicion.

Almost the same can be said for car badges. There are several companies that re-enamel badges and, although much of their work is of a high standard, a badge so treated will look new and fresh and, if displayed with other, more original badges, will stand out like a sore thumb. Polychrome enamel, with its luminescent quality, was frequently used before the Second World War, particularly on prestige badges, but it is easily chipped, and replacement today is very expensive. It is much better to buy a badge showing its age, with all the scratches and signs of wear it has acquired over the years. On the other hand, a particularly rare but damaged item that would be otherwise difficult to find is fair game for the restorer. It must also be remembered that replating a mascot or re-enamelling a badge will affect its market value, possibly reducing it by as much as half. Take care with your collecting and your collection will take care of you.

Collecting sources

Once you have decided to collect either motoring mascots or badges (or both!), the first thing you should do is to start handling them. In this way you can judge for yourself the relative qualities, the colour, the feel and texture, and you will begin to get a sense of the patination that only time and antiquity can generate. One way of experiencing this is to attend one of the many Autojumbles – the motoring equivalent of the antique fairs – which are advertised throughout the year. The largest of these is the National Motor Museum Autojumble, which takes place at Beaulieu, near Southampton, every September. There you can talk to stallholders, handle their goods, compare qualities and arrive at your own conclusions about their acceptability, bearing in mind your budget.

Similar opportunities present themselves during an Automobilia auction sale preview. Do not be put off by the apparent haughtiness of the larger auction houses. Stake your claim to service, as you may be good money-earning potential for them. Do not be afraid to ask questions. Inspect the property on offer; benefit by asking questions of others, perhaps fellow customers, who are often more knowledgeable; then sit back and watch the sale – all this for gratis. Then, after a period of investigation, decide on your collecting theme, which can be as imaginative as you like. I know a man who collects enamel badges only featuring the county of Kent; my sister-in-law collects French mascots; another old motoring sage of my acquaintance goes for those depicting scantily clad women; all enjoy their collecting, and all enjoy the camaraderie of other collectors. Always purchase the best you can afford, as quality rather than quantity is of paramount importance, but, above all, enjoy the experience.

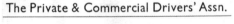

The Private & Commercial Drivers' Assn.

THE HALL MARK

OF EFFICIENCY.

BADGE (Three-quarter size.)

Not a badge but a promotional postcard advertising The Private and Commercial Drivers' Association, a club formed to foster courteous driving of commercial vehicles and encouraging the public to report bad driving, the forerunner of present-day vehicles emblazoned 'How's My Driving? Please Phone....'.

Further reading

Titles marked * are highly recommended.

*Gardiner, Gordon, and Morris, Alistair. *Automobilia of Europe: Reference and Price Guide*. The Antique Collectors' Club, 1982 and 1995.
Huntsburger, Lynn. *U.S. Hood Ornaments and More*. Prairie Land Publishing, Illinois, 1994.
Kay, David, and Springate, Lynda. *Automotive Mascots: A Collector's Guide to British Marque, Corporate and Accessory Mascots*. Veloce Publishing, 1999.
*Legrand, Michel. *Mascottes Automobiles*. C Editions, 1993.
*Legrand, Michel. *Mascottes Passion*. Antic Show, 1999.
Martells, Jack. *Antique Automotive Collectibles*. Contemporary Books, Inc., Chicago, 1980.
Moto-Meter: A Listing of Vintage Original Master Artwork Nameplate Renderings for the Moto-Meter Company. COHASCO, Automobiliana & History of Transportation.
Nicholson, T. R. *Car Badges of the World*. Cassell, 1970. (Radiator badges)
Passmore, Michael. *The AA: History, Badges and Memorabilia*. Shire, 2003.
*Särnesjö, Jan. *World of Car Badges*. Darwin Books, 2003.
Sirignano, G., and Sulzberger, D. *Car Mascots*. Macdonald & James, 1977.
Smith, Dan. *Accessory Mascots: The Automotive Accents of Yesteryear 1910–1940*. Dan Smith, 1989.
Williams, William C. *Motoring Mascots of the World*. Motorbooks International, second edition 1998.
Williamson, Joan. *Badges of the Royal Automobile Club*. Royal Automobile Club, 1999.
Worthington-Williams, Michael. *Automobilia: A Guided Tour for Collectors*. B. T. Batsford and the Royal Automobile Club, 1979.

The Key to the Open Road

The Automobile Association was the first club to offer assistance with road patrols, introduced in 1905, and, later, roadside telephone boxes, for which a key was supplied. These keys, of various designs, are highly collectable today and will add an extra dimension to any display of badges. The image also reminds us of the AA maxim 'When a patrol man does not salute, stop and ask the reason why', the reason often being that speed police were in the area.

Places to visit

Many motoring museums have mascots and badges on display, where they are usually fitted to motor vehicles. Although this is an appropriate concept, it is unfortunate that seldom does the mascot or badge get a mention on the motor vehicle information plaque. Sometimes mascots and badges are inappropriately fitted, frequently being treated by the museum staff as a picturesque adjunct, rather than a historical feature. On the other hand the National Motor Museum at Beaulieu, like a number of other international institutions, not only has mascots and badges attached to museum vehicles but also has an archive selection that the public can view if a request is made in advance of a visit. The museums listed below are known to have a good selection of mascots and badges available for inspection.

Beamish, The North of England Open Air Museum, Beamish, County Durham DH9 0RG. Telephone: 0191 370 4000. Website: www.beamish.org.uk

British Motor Industries Heritage Centre, Banbury Road, Gaydon, Warwickshire CV35 0BJ. Telephone: 01926 641188. Website: www.heritage.org.uk

Cotswold Motor Museum, The Old Mill, Bourton-on-the-Water, Gloucestershire GL54 2BY. Telephone: 01451 821255. Website: www.cotswold-motor-museum.com

Coventry Transport Museum, Millennium Place, Hales Street, Coventry CV1 1PN. Telephone: 024 7683 2465. Website: www.transport-museum.com

Museum of Irish Transport, Scotts Hotel Gardens, Killarney, County Kerry, Ireland. Telephone: 00353 (0) 64 32638. Website: www.gleneaglehotel.com/transmues.htm

National Motor Museum, John Montagu Building, Beaulieu, Brockenhurst, Hampshire SO42 7ZN. Telephone: 01590 612345. Website: www.beaulieu.co.uk

National Museum of Scotland, Chambers Street, Edinburgh EH1 1JF. Telephone: 0131 247 4422. Website: www.nms.ac.uk

A Humber 11 horsepower Drop Head Coupé of c.1918 sporting an Automobile Association club badge attached to the front radiator grille, an Augustine and Emile Lejeune 'Speed Nymph' naked female mascot on the radiator cap and an unusually positioned RAC Associate's Badge for the Midland Car Club mounted on the roof above the windscreen. Clearly, this owner-driver wanted his loyalties on display.

Index